COMPANIONS *in Christ*

A SMALL-GROUP EXPERIENCE IN SPIRITUAL FORMATION

D1358371

RESPONDING
~ *to* OUR CALL

Participant's Book | Volume 4

Gerritt Scott Dawson

UPPER
ROOM BOOKS®
NASHVILLE

COMPANIONS IN CHRIST
RESPONDING TO OUR CALL: THE WORK OF CHRIST
Participant's Book: Part 4
Copyright © 2006 by Upper Room Books®
All rights reserved.

Upper Room Books® website: books.upperroom.org

UPPER ROOM®, UPPER ROOM BOOKS® and design logos are trademarks owned by the Upper Room®, Nashville, Tennessee. All rights reserved.

At the time of publication all websites referenced in this book were valid. However, due to the fluid nature of the Internet some addresses may have changed or the content may no longer be relevant.

Cover design: Left Coast Design, Portland, OR
Cover photo: Adri Berger; Stone/Getty Images
Interior icon development: Michael C. McGuire, settingPace

ISBN 978-0-8358-9833-1

Contents

Acknowledgments

Companions in Christ is truly the result of the efforts of a team of persons who shared a common vision. This team graciously contributed their knowledge and experience to develop a small-group resource that would creatively engage persons in a journey of spiritual growth and discovery. The author of Part 4 was Gerrit Scott Dawson. Stephen Bryant was the primary author of the daily exercises and the Leader's Guide. Marjorie Thompson created the original design and participated in the editing of the entire resource. Keith Beasley-Topliffe served as a consultant in the creation of the process for the small-group meetings and contributed numerous ideas that influenced the final shape of the resource. In the early stages of development, two advisory groups read and responded to the initial drafts of material. The persons participating as members of those advisory groups were Jeannette Bakke, Avery Brooke, Thomas Parker, Helen Pearson Smith, Luther E. Smith Jr., Eradio Valverde Jr., Diane Luton Blum, Carol Bumbalough, Ruth Torri, and Mark Wilson. Prior to publication, test groups in the following churches used the material and provided helpful suggestions for improvement of the Participant's Books and the Leader's Guide.

First United Methodist Church, Hartselle, Alabama
St. George's Episcopal Church, Nashville, Tennessee

Northwest Presbyterian Church, Atlanta, Georgia
Garfield Memorial United Methodist Church,
    Pepper Pike, Ohio
First United Methodist Church, Corpus Christi, Texas
Malibu United Methodist Church, Malibu, California
First United Methodist Church, Santa Monica, California
St. Paul United Methodist Church, San Antonio, Texas
Trinity Presbyterian Church, Arvada, Colorado
First United Methodist Church, Franklin, Tennessee
La Trinidad United Methodist Church, San Antonio, Texas
Aldersgate United Methodist Church, Slidell, Louisiana

My deep gratitude goes to all these persons and groups for their contribution to and support of *Companions in Christ*.

—Janice T. Grana, editor of *Companions in Christ*
April 2001

Introduction

Welcome to Part 4 of Companions in Christ, a small-group resource for spiritual formation. This resource is designed to create a setting where you can respond to God's call to an ever-deepening communion and wholeness in Christ—as an individual, as a member of a small group, and as part of a congregation. The resource focuses on your experience of God and your discovery of spiritual practices that help you share more fully in the life of Christ. You will be exploring the potential of Christian community as an environment of grace and mutual guidance through the Spirit. You will grow closer to members of your small group as you seek together to know and respond to God's will. And your congregation will grow when you and your companions begin to bring what you learn into all areas of church life, from classes and meetings to worship and outreach.

How does *Companions in Christ* help you grow spiritually? It enables you to immerse yourself in "streams of living waters" through the spiritual disciplines of prayer, scripture, ministry, worship, study, and Christian conversation. These means of grace are the common ways in which Christ meets people, renews their faith, and deepens their life together in love. In the first part of *Companions in Christ* you were introduced to the concept of spiritual formation as a journey. In the second part you explored the depths of scripture. In the third part of *Companions in Christ,* you experienced new dimensions of prayer. In this fourth unit, you will reflect on Christ's call in your life and discover anew the gifts that God is giving you for living out your personal ministry.

In the last unit, you and members of your group will grow together as a Christian community and gain skills in learning how small groups in the church become settings for spiritual guidance.

Although *Companions* is not an introductory course in Christianity for new Christians, it will help church people take up the basic disciplines of faith in renewing and transforming ways.

An Outline of the Resource

Companions in Christ has two primary components: individual reading and daily exercises throughout the week with this Participant's Book and a weekly two-hour meeting based on suggestions in the Leader's Guide. For each week, the Participant's Book has a chapter introducing new material and five daily exercises to help you reflect on your life in light of the content of the chapter. After the Preparatory Meeting of your group, you will begin a weekly cycle as follows: On day 1 you will be asked to read the chapter and on days 2–6 to complete the five daily exercises (found at the end of the chapter reading). On day 7 you will meet with your group. The daily exercises aim to help you move from information (knowledge about) to experience (knowledge of). An important part of this process is keeping a personal notebook or journal where you record reflections, prayers, and questions for later review and for reference at the weekly group meeting. The time commitment for the daily exercises is about thirty minutes. The weekly meeting will include time for reflecting on the exercises of the past week, for moving deeper into learnings from chapter readings, for having group experiences of prayer, and for considering ways to share with the congregation what you have learned or experienced.

The complete material in *Companions in Christ* covers a period of twenty-eight weeks divided into five parts or units, of which this volume is the fourth. The five parts are as follows:

1. *Embracing the Journey: The Way of Christ* (five weeks)—a basic exploration of spiritual formation as a journey toward wholeness and holiness, individually and in community, through the grace of God.

2. *Feeding on the Word: The Mind of Christ* (five weeks)—an introduction to several ways of meditating on and praying with scripture.

3. *Deepening Our Prayer: The Heart of Christ* (six weeks)—a guided experience of various forms and styles of prayer.

4. *Responding to Our Call: The Work of Christ* (five weeks)—a presentation of vocation or call: giving ourselves to God in willing obedience and receiving the fruits and gifts of the Holy Spirit.

5. *Exploring Spiritual Guidance: The Spirit of Christ* (five weeks)— an overview of different ways of giving and receiving spiritual guidance, from one-on-one relationships, to spiritual growth groups, to guidance in congregational life as a whole.

Your group may want to take a short break between units either to allow for some unstructured reflection time or to avoid meeting near Christmas or Easter. However, the units are designed to be sequential—each unit builds on previous ones.

This Participant's Book includes an annotated resource list that describes additional books related to the theme of this part of *Companions in Christ*.

You will need to bring your Participant's Book, your Bible, and your personal notebook or journal to the weekly group meeting.

Your Personal Notebook or Journal

"I began these pages for myself, in order to think out my own particular pattern of living. . . . And since I think best with a pencil in my hand, I started naturally to write." Anne Morrow Lindbergh began her beloved classic, *Gift from the Sea*, with these words. You may not imagine that you "think best with a pencil in hand," but there is something truly wonderful about what can happen when we reflect on the inner life through writing.

Keeping a journal or personal notebook (commonly called journaling) will be one of the most important dimensions of your personal experience with *Companions in Christ*. The Participant's Book gives you daily spiritual exercises every week. More often than not, you will be asked to note your thoughts, reflections, questions, feelings, or prayers in relation to the exercises.

Even if you are totally inexperienced in this kind of personal writing, you may find that it becomes second nature very quickly. Your thoughts may start to pour out of you, giving expression to an inner life that has never been released. If, on the other hand, you find the writing difficult or cumbersome, give yourself permission to try it in a new way. Because a journal is "for your eyes only," you may choose any style that suits you. You need not worry about making your words sound beautiful or about writing with good grammar and spelling. You don't even need to write complete sentences! Jotting down key ideas, insights, or musings is just fine. You might want to doodle while you think or sketch an image that comes to you. Make journaling fun and relaxed. No one will see what you write, and you have complete freedom to share with the group only what you choose of your reflections.

There are two important reasons for keeping a journal or personal notebook as you move through *Companions in Christ*. First, the process of writing down our thoughts clarifies them for us. They become more specific and concrete. Sometimes we really do not know what we think until we see our thoughts on paper, and often the process of writing itself generates new creative insight. Second, this personal record captures what we have been experiencing inwardly over time. Journaling helps us track changes in our thinking and growth of insight. Our memories are notoriously fragile and fleeting in this regard. Specific feelings or creative connections we may have had two weeks ago, or even three days ago, are hard to recall without a written record. Even though your journal cannot capture all that goes through your mind in a single reflection period, it will serve as a reminder. You will need to draw on these reminders during small-group meetings each week.

Begin by purchasing a book that you can use for this purpose. It can be as simple as a spiral-bound notebook or as fancy as a cloth-bound blank book. Some people prefer lined paper and some unlined. You will want, at minimum, something more permanent than a ring-binder or paper pad. The Upper Room has made available a companion journal for this resource that you can purchase if you so desire. Or you can use the blank pages at the back of this book.

When you begin the daily exercises, have your journal and pen or pencil at hand. You need not wait until you have finished reading and thinking an exercise through completely. Learn to stop and write as you go. Think on paper. Feel free to write anything that comes to you, even if it seems to be "off the topic." It may turn out to be more relevant or useful than you first think. If the process seems clumsy at first, don't fret. Like any spiritual practice, it gets easier over time, and its value becomes more apparent.

Here is how your weekly practice of journaling is shaped. On the first day after your group meeting, read the new chapter. Jot down your responses to the reading: "aha" moments, questions, points of disagreement, images, or any other reflections you wish to record. You may prefer to note these in the margins of the chapter. Over the next five days, you will do the exercises for the week, recording either general or specific responses as they are invited. On the day of the group meeting, it will be helpful to review what you have written through the week, perhaps marking portions you would like to share in the group. Bring your journal with you to meetings so that you can refer to it directly or refresh your memory of significant moments you want to paraphrase during discussion times. With time, you may indeed find that journaling helps you to think out your own pattern of living and that you will be able to see more clearly how God is at work in your life.

Your Group Meeting

The weekly group meeting is divided into four segments. First you will gather for a brief time of worship and prayer. This offers an opportunity to set aside the many concerns of the day and center on God's presence and guidance as you begin your group session.

The second section of the meeting is called "Sharing Insights." During this time you will be invited to talk about your experiences with the daily exercises. The group leader will participate as a member and share his or her responses as well. Generally the sharing by each member will be brief and related to specific exercises. This is an important time for your group to learn and practice what it means to be a community of persons seeking to listen to God and to live more faithfully as disciples of Christ. The group provides a supportive space to explore your listening, your spiritual practices, and how you are attempting to put those practices into daily life. Group members need not comment or offer advice to one another. Rather the group members help you, by their attentiveness and prayer, to pay attention to what has been happening in your particular response to the daily exercises. The group is not functioning as a traditional support group that offers suggestions or help to one another. Rather, the group members trust that the Holy Spirit is the guide and that they are called to help one another listen to that guidance.

The "Sharing Insights" time presents a unique opportunity to learn how God works differently in each of our lives. Our journeys, while varied, are enriched by others' experiences. We can hold one another in prayer, and we can honor each other's experience. Through this part of the meeting, you will see in fresh ways how God's activity may touch or address our lives in unexpected ways. The group will need to establish some ground rules to facilitate the sharing. For example, you may want to be clear that each person speak only about his or her own beliefs, feelings, and responses and that all group members have permission to share only what and when they are ready to share. Above all, the group needs to maintain confidentiality so that what is shared in the group stays in the group. This part of the group meeting will be much less meaningful if persons interrupt and try to comment on what is being said or try to "fix" what they see as a problem. The leader will close this part of the meeting by calling attention to any patterns or themes that seem to emerge from the group's sharing. These patterns may point to a word that God is offering to the group. Notice that the group leader functions both as a participant and as someone who aids the process by listening and summarizing the key insights that have surfaced.

The third segment of the group meeting is called "Deeper Explorations." This part of the meeting may expand on ideas contained in the week's chapter, offer practice in the spiritual disciplines introduced in the chapter or exercises, or give group members a chance to reflect on the implications of what they are learning for themselves and for their church. It offers a common learning experience for the group and a chance to go deeper in our understanding of how we can share more fully in the mind, heart, and work of Jesus Christ.

As it began, the group meeting ends with a brief time of worship, an ideal time for the group to share special requests for intercession that might come from the conversation and experience of the meeting or other prayer requests that arise naturally from the group.

The weeks that you participate in *Companions in Christ* will offer you the opportunity to focus on your relationship with Christ and to grow in your openness to God's presence and guidance. The unique aspect of this experience is that members of your small group, who are indeed your companions on the journey, will encourage your searching and learning. Those of us who have written and edited this resource offer our prayers that God will speak to you during these weeks and awaken you to enlarged possibilities of love and service in Christ's name. As we listen and explore together, we will surely meet our loving God who waits eagerly to guide us toward deeper maturity in Christ by the gracious working of the Holy Spirit.

Part 4

Responding to Our Call: The Work of Christ

Gerrit Scott Dawson

Part 4, Week 1
Radical Availability

*S*o, what am I supposed to do now? This question arises for many of us after we accept Christ's invitation to follow him in the journey of the spiritual life. After we have read the scriptures, meditated on them, and prayed, the new day stretches out before us. What do Christians do?

In Part 4 of *Companions in Christ*, we will consider the idea of vocation—what God calls us to be and do in the world. Each of us has a unique combination of personality traits and gifts. When we are able to put into practice the design that God has put within us, we find high levels of energy, fulfillment, and purpose. Ideally, what we are to do as Christians is to live in loving service to God in the world, according to the way we were created. We share in the ministry of Jesus who gave himself completely to us.

As this theme unfolds, we will explore what it means that God has given each of us a spiritual gift to use in our work with Christ. Ultimately, I hope each of us will discover a joyful, invigorating role in the church through which we may exercise our gifts in concert with others to the praise of God. That is where we want to go; but to get there, we have to do some essential work first.

In our society, questions concerning vocation seem natural. We live in a culture that greatly values self-fulfillment. I believe that living in alignment with God's purposes for us is the surest path to such

satisfaction. But discovering our call and exercising our gifts are not of first importance in the Christian life. They cannot be, because most Christians have not had the freedom or power to make many choices about the circumstances of their lives. The slaves, the women, and the working poor who comprised so much of the early church had little say in their vocational choices. The primary call of God to us, then, must be audible in all stages, conditions, and seasons of life. This call is profoundly simple, yet, as T. S. Eliot wrote in *Four Quartets*, answering it costs "not less than everything." Moreover, the successful discovery of our gifts and particular calling depends upon our acceptance of this primal summons from God.

Many stories in the Bible describe how people are called to particular service. In each case, there is a basic call around which all the other details of life swirl like harmony around a strong melody. Persons are called to abandon their lives completely into God's hands. There is just no way around this. A test precedes any consideration of what you are to do in the world: Have you let go of everything to give yourself to God? Again and again, the people we encounter in the Bible are called to a radical availability. God shakes them free of every other constraint so that they trust only in their Lord. Then the vision of a particular service and the power to do it can be given.

Oswald Chambers in his book *My Utmost for His Highest* has written of the "gracious uncertainty" that "marks the spiritual life":

> To be certain of God means that we are uncertain in all our ways, we do not know what a day may bring forth. This is generally said with a sigh of sadness; it should be rather an expression of breathless expectation. We are uncertain of the next step, but we are certain of God. Immediately we abandon to God, and do the duty that lies nearest. [God] packs our life with surprises all the time.[1]

We are called to love the Lord our God with all our heart, soul, and mind. Our certainty rests only in God. The priority of God can entertain no division between spiritual life and work life, family time and recreation time. God commands; God calls for first place in every aspect. From such basic commitment and truth arises every other consideration of vocation.

At every moment we practice a surrender that has no limits, a surrender that includes all possible methods and degrees of service to God. . . . Our sole duty is to submit ourselves to all that God sends us and to stand ready to do [God's] will at all times.

—Jean-Pierre de Caussade

This week we will consider several stories of biblical characters and how they followed the first call of committing all to God. We will see that sometimes this primal vocation involves literal abandonment of all we have. At times it means willingness to put our present positions at risk. And at times we continue in the same life but for a whole new reason. In every case, our first call involves embracing the "gracious uncertainty" that follows saying yes to God.

Abram and Sarai

The story of Abram and Sarai marks the beginning of a new phase in God's expression of love for a wayward humanity. These two were to begin a lineage of people called apart from the world in order to be a blessing to the world. At first, the call came to Abram alone:

> Now the LORD said to Abram, "Go from your country and your kindred and your father's house to the land that I will show you. I will make of you a great nation, and I will bless you, and make your name great, so that you will be a blessing. . . . In you all the families of the earth shall be blessed." So Abram went, as the LORD had told him (Gen. 12:1-4).

The first call was to leave familiar and beloved territory—his country, his extended family, and his father's house. He was not required to give up everything, for he traveled with his wife Sarai, his nephew Lot, and all his servants and possessions. And with the call, God made great promises: Abram's family would grow into a populous nation, and the entire earth would be blessed through him. But to reach the goal, he had to set out for a destination known only as "the land that I will show you." At age seventy-five, Abram had to uproot his personal household and journey blindly to "God knows where." Everything familiar was shaken loose. He was certain only of God.

Esther

Esther, a Jewish woman, became queen of Persia during the reign of Xerxes (486–465 B.C.E.). During those days, a large number of God's people who had been scattered during the Exile a century earlier still

lived in foreign lands. No one in the Persian court knew of Esther's faith or heritage. She had been discovered during a royal search for a new queen after the old one had enraged the king by daring to defy him. Esther's beauty and graciousness overwhelmed Xerxes.

Meanwhile, one of the king's officials, in a personal fury at Esther's cousin Mordecai, convinced the king to sign an order to exterminate all the Hebrews in the land. Mordecai sent a message to Esther, urging her to intercede with the king on behalf of her people. But Esther understood the ways of the court and the temper of the king. She sent word back to Mordecai reminding him that the penalty for approaching the king unbidden was death. Mordecai replied with a message that surely was no less than a call from God:

> Do not think that in the king's palace you will escape any more than all the other Jews. For if you keep silence at such a time as this, relief and deliverance will rise for the Jews from another quarter, but you and your father's family will perish. Who knows? Perhaps you have come to royal dignity for just such a time as this (Esth. 4:13-14).

This prophetic word identifies several important aspects of God's call. First, Mordecai reminded Esther of her deepest identity as one of God's own people. Then he boldly asserted how dangerous this moment of call was for her. He did not veil the threat. In the critical hour of opportunity, if she sought to save her life, she would surely lose it. Third, Mordecai asserted the fulfillment of God's purposes even without her cooperation. God would be faithful to the Hebrews, passing over Esther and using another means to save them. Finally, Mordecai asked Esther to consider that her new, elevated station in life had been given to her for precisely this moment. She was given a royal position not to preserve it at all costs but to risk it in response to God's call.

Esther was not only beautiful in appearance. She was a woman of extraordinary strength and courage. She heard God's call in Mordecai's words and sent this reply: "Go, gather all the Jews to be found in Susa, and hold a fast on my behalf. . . . I and my maids will also fast as you do. After that I will go to the king, though it is against the law; and if I perish, I perish" (Esth. 4:16). She called for prayer and support from all of God's people. But Esther also resolved to do what she alone could do. Her courage was built on a complete abandonment to the care of God. "If I perish, I perish." She held back nothing, risking not only wealth and comfort but also her very life. And she succeeded. The king received her favorably, lifted the edict, and ultimately elevated the status of all the Jews in Persia.

Jesus' Answer to God's Call

Jesus' ministry was characterized by radical availability, both to his Father in heaven and to those around him. He began his public life by submitting to John's baptism of repentance, though he himself was without sin. Interestingly, such an act of availability led immediately to a sign of confirmation. The Gospels tell us that as he came out of the water, the Holy Spirit descended upon him in the form of a dove, and a voice from heaven spoke, "This is my Son, the Beloved, with whom I am well pleased" (Matt. 3:17). God the Father affirmed the nature and work of the Son as his public ministry began.

In a succinct but profound way, this story reveals the reality that God is triune; such knowledge will deeply inform our explorations throughout the coming weeks. The voice from heaven, that of God the Father, announces to the world that Jesus is the Father's beloved Son. From all eternity, the Father and the Son have existed in a relationship of love so intimate that they could be called one. Throughout his life with us, Jesus constantly prayed to his Father, revealing that though he had become human, his oneness in communion with God remained. The Holy Spirit who descended upon Jesus is also one with God and has been known as the very bond of the Trinity. That Jesus should teach us to begin our prayers with "Our Father . . ." is nothing less than an invitation to all humanity to join in the wonderful fellowship of love that defines God!

Throughout the three years of his ministry, Jesus was constantly accessible to God's call, spending vast amounts of time in prayer. Mark recalls the time when, "in the morning, while it was still very dark, [Jesus] got up and went out to a deserted place, and there he prayed" (1:35). And Luke tells us, "Now during those days he went out

to the mountain to pray; and he spent the night in prayer to God" (6:12). Such devotion allowed Jesus to say, "I have come . . . , not to do my own will, but the will of him who sent me" (John 6:38).

Jesus' intimate relationship with God flowed forth from prayer into his works of compassion. His life of healing can be summarized in his simple words to the centurion whose servant lay near death, "I will come and cure him" (Matt. 8:7). It was his will to be interrupted by the needs of others and to meet those needs with his healing, forgiving love. Constantly welcoming outcasts, Jesus declared, "I have come to call not the righteous but sinners" (Matt. 9:13).

Such obedience to God led Jesus into conflict. He said of the laws of Moses, "I have come not to abolish but to fulfill [them]" (Matt. 5:17). Yet Jesus' healing on the Sabbath and overturning the money tables in the Temple scandalized the religious leaders. Although they sought his life, Jesus continued his ministry of love.

Jesus' willing obedience continued even though betrayal and death lay ahead. Several times, we read that he predicted his death. And praying in the garden of Gethsemane, Jesus acknowledged the end he was facing. In his true humanity, he hoped to avoid the suffering; but as Immanuel, God with us in radical availability, he gave himself to God: "My Father, if it is possible, let this cup pass from me; yet not what I want, but what you want" (Matt. 26:39). The essence of abandonment followed as Jesus gave his life on the cross.

Jesus' Call to the Disciples

Jesus called his followers to a similar life of obedience as part of their intimate relationship with him. The Gospels record Jesus calling one person after another to this radical availability. "Follow me," he said to Simon Peter and Andrew, "and I will make you fish for people" (Mark 1:17). They immediately left their nets to follow Jesus. Shortly thereafter, Jesus called James and John. They left not only their nets but also their father sitting in the boat! "Follow me," Jesus said to Levi the tax collector; Levi got up and left his coins in the tax booth (Mark 2:14). Like Abram, these early disciples were called to an unknown

Jesus came to the "far country" because he was sent. Being sent remained uppermost in his consciousness. He never claimed anything for himself. He was the obedient servant who said and did nothing, absolutely nothing, unless it was said and done in complete obedience to the one who sent him.

—Douglas P. McNeill,
Douglas A. Morrison,
Henri J. M. Nouwen

destination. All they knew was the person Jesus, and he provided their only certainty. This bond with Jesus, forged in radical availability, brought closer ties than those of family: "Here are my mother and my brothers! For whoever does the will of my Father in heaven is my brother and sister and mother" (Matt. 12:49-50).

A rich young man came to Jesus inquiring about eternal life. Mark records Jesus' call that paid little respect to the man's wealth:

> Jesus, looking at him, loved him and said, "You lack one thing; go, sell what you own, and give the money to the poor, and you will have treasure in heaven; then come, follow me." When he heard this, he was shocked and went away grieving, for he had many possessions (10:21-22).

The demands on the young man felt overwhelming. Jesus made it clear to his disciples, in words that echo Mordecai's to Esther, "If any want to become my followers, let them deny themselves and take up their cross and follow me. For those who want to save their life will lose it, and those who lose their life for my sake, and for the sake of the gospel, will save it" (Mark 8:34-35).

Only out of this total yes to his call can Jesus' followers begin to share his work. We may hold nothing back. Everything is subject to forfeit. And the essence of this call and response is the Great Commandment, "Love the Lord your God with all your heart, and with all your soul, and with all your mind, and with all your strength" (Mark 12:30).

Lydia

Those of us who find such demands from Jesus daunting may find solace in the story of Lydia. A merchant who heard the call of Christ and heeded it obediently, Lydia did not leave home or change profession:

> A certain woman named Lydia, a worshiper of God, was listening to us; she was from the city of Thyatira and a dealer in purple cloth. The Lord opened her heart to listen eagerly to what was said by Paul. When she and her household were baptized, she urged us, saying, "If you have judged me to be faithful to the Lord, come and stay at my home" (Acts 16:14-15).

You aspire to live dangerously for the sake of Christ. Each day you will ask yourself the meaning of his word, "Whoever wants to save their life will lose it." And one day you will understand what this absolute means.

How will you come to understand? Search. Seek and you will find.

—Brother Roger of Taizé

Lydia abandoned herself to God in her baptism, yet continued in her prosperous profession. Now, however, she uses her resources to become the host for the church in Thyatira. At the end of Acts 16, we read that Paul and Silas leave prison and accept Lydia's invitation of hospitality. There they find a flourishing fellowship of brothers and sisters in the Lord (Acts 16:40). Everything changed for Lydia, but her external circumstances remained the same. She followed a deeper vocation while maintaining the same professional duties.

So we see that heeding God's call can mean leaving home and all that is familiar. It can demand our accumulated wealth and security or dare us to place our blessings, even our lives, at risk. It can also mean simply living where we are but with an entirely new set of priorities. In every case, our particular vocation in God's service arises from our response to the basic call to radical availability.

DAILY EXERCISES

Be sure to read the chapter "Radical Availability" before you begin these exercises. Keep a journal or blank book beside you to record your thoughts, questions, prayers, and images.

This week's exercises will give you an opportunity to begin reflecting on your calling or vocation in life.

EXERCISE 1

This week's chapter considered several stories of biblical characters (Abram and Sarai, Esther, Jesus, Jesus' disciples, and Lydia) and how they followed the first call of committing all to God. Which of their stories is more like your story, and in what ways? Meditate on the scripture passage related to the character of your choice. Identify connections with your experience and your own God-given opportunities. Pray to the Lord to open your heart and to give you courage for the next step in your journey.

EXERCISE 2

Read Luke 10:25-37. This story reveals the quality of life and love that God wants to give us. What kind of life do you want to inherit? Spend time in prayer with the phrase "Do this, and you will live." What specifically is the Lord calling you to do?

EXERCISE 3

Read Isaiah 6:1-13. Isaiah experienced God's presence and call in the course of Temple worship. Do as Isaiah did here: Outline in your journal the story of your first sense of God's calling and your response ("Here am I; send me"). Drawing on your experience, describe what "God's call" means for you.

EXERCISE 4

Read Mark 10:17-22. Meditate on Jesus' words to the rich man as words to you. What area of your life have you closed off to God's call and, as good as it seems by all external standards, may prevent you from

receiving the life God wants to give you? In prayer, risk placing your whole life, including all of your achievements, in God's hands. Rest in the assurance that Jesus loves you and knows you as you are. Record your insights.

EXERCISE 5

Read Psalm 103. Meditate on God's nature as expressed in this psalm, and bless God's holy name with your own affirmations. Identify the verses that touch your spirit and resonate most deeply with the work and call of God in you. How do these verses about God speak to you of your vocation in God? Pray through the psalm verses that especially draw you, blessing God's holy name with all that is in you. Receive and rest in the blessing of God's presence.

Review your journal for the week in preparation for the group meeting.

Part 4, Week 2
Living Reliance

*L*ast week I may have set you up for failure or at least created some anxiety about what God calls you to do. We looked at stories of people who risked everything for God. Perhaps you felt, as I did, that the faithfulness of Abram, Esther, Jesus, and the disciples differs greatly from our own. I realized that quite often I make myself unavailable to God. I may say that I offer myself but then proceed to do just what I want anyway. Rarely do I live in obedience to God's call for any sustained length of time. Radical availability seems like radical impossibility! Trying to work together with Christ becomes one more heavy stone on my pile of guilt. But what if God has anticipated this very sense of failure, which serves in fact as an unexpected beginning to joyful participation in the life and work of Jesus?

Last week we saw that when Jesus called the rich young ruler to radical availability, the man "was shocked and went away grieving, for he had many possessions" (Mark 10:22). Jesus went on to comment, "Children, how hard it is to enter the kingdom of God!" His words astounded the disciples. If the rich and successful were not in God's favor, then who was? They asked, "Then who can be saved?"

Jesus replied, "For mortals it is impossible, but not for God; for God, all things are possible." Jesus understood that we cannot of our own power generate or sustain our radical availability to God. Consistently working with Christ to enter the kingdom of God is not

humanly attainable. God calls us then to more than we can do on our own.

We stand at the threshold of a paradoxical truth in the spiritual life: At precisely the point where we abandon ourselves to God, we realize we have done nothing by our own power. When we feel we have accomplished the Herculean task of giving over everything—all control, all claim, all ambition—we discover that God gets all the credit. God enables our will, quickens our belief, empowers our service. Our availability, while crucial, is but the tiniest step; even that step is not taken without divine prompting and enabling.

Last week we noted Jesus' perfect availability to God. Out of his life of prayerful communion with God, Jesus taught with wisdom and healed with power. He also summoned others to follow him in abandonment to God. We are called to be like him. Yet we know that we cannot be like him. "For mortals it is impossible." Jesus, while mortal, also was and is much more. He is Immanuel, God with us. Jesus is God incarnate, come in the flesh. So while fully human, he is also fully divine, the "exact imprint of God's very being" (Heb. 1:3). And "for God, all things are possible." Only Jesus, who bears the titles Son of Man and Son of God, can empower us to share in the life of radical availability that he lived as a human being.

To share in the work of Christ means not so much our working for Christ but our inviting him to work in and through us. We cease trying to be in ourselves what he is and agree to his living in us all that he is as both human being and God. We grow toward that spiritual reality named by Paul in his letter to the Galatians, "It is no longer I who live, but it is Christ who lives in me" (2:20).

Thus, we may not frame the whole subject of what we are to do in the world, what our mission is, in terms of ourselves. Rather, we consider our life's task in terms of Jesus Christ. The issue is not my spiritual journey and my quest for God. That's backward. What matters is God's quest for me, indeed, God's quest for the whole world. The Son of God came down from heaven seeking us. That's what counts. Who Jesus is then becomes the most important consideration in determining what you and I are to do.

I am depending too utterly on my own strength. I act as if my knowledge were complete and my own power sufficient. I forget to remember that God is my strength and the source of the power without which no thing is possible. . . . There is strength in God sufficient for my needs, whatever they may be.

—Howard Thurman

We would be wise not to get ahead of this understanding. Even mighty works in the name of Christ will come to nothing if they are not grounded in this essential order: not I, but Christ; not me for God, but God for and through me. When we make this connection, then even the smallest actions by the most limited of people become great contributions to the kingdom.

The Vine and the Branches

Jesus gave us a powerful symbol in John 15 for this relationship of participating in the work of God. The image is that of a grapevine. The thick, long vine grows along the ground or attaches itself by tendrils to another tree or a frame. From the vine, little branches shoot out, intertwining as they climb. From these branches the clusters of grapes come forth. A cultivated grapevine may grow very long and high, with many bunches of fruit hanging down.

The grapevine had long been a symbol for Israel, God's people. Commentator Ray Summers notes that on the temple in Jerusalem, a huge grapevine was carved into the stone of the entrance.[1] Its trunk rose higher than a person, and its branches spread out farther above, adorned with rich gold leaves and bunches of gilded grapes. Moreover, during the brief time of Israel's revolt against Rome, the coins minted bore the grapevine as the symbol of the nation. The grapevine served as an image of hope that the people could be something fruitful for their God.

But in reality, the grapevine became a reminder of failure. The Hebrew prophets often employed this figure of speech in terms of judgment (see Isaiah 5:1-10): Israel, the vine that had not produced the fruit God expected. Instead of choice fruit, wild grapes had sprung forth, worthless either for wine or food. God's people, by their own efforts, could not fulfill their task in the world.

Jesus, however, employed the symbol in a new way. Summers suggests that the conversation recorded in John 15, on the night before the crucifixion, may have taken place near the Temple, under the light of the Passover moon, with its beams shining upon the engraved vine

on the temple entrance. Here Jesus said, "I am the vine, you are the branches" (John 15:5). This understanding is crucial. Jesus took Israel's place. He stood in for God's people as the one who is expected to produce the fruit of obedience, worship, and faithfulness. In effect, Jesus said, "I am that vine on the Temple. I have come to be the source, the very plant that produces fruit for God. Now you are the branches that grow from me, the vine. You are the tiny shoots that come forth and in due season bear the grapes. So stay connected to me."

Jesus' image was stunningly obvious. Branches don't try to live apart from the vine. They are just there, effortlessly letting the vine produce its life through them, resulting in a harvest of grapes. No branch leaps off the tree. No branch tries to do anything. Branches simply remain, held by the vine, yielding fruit. We are to do the same.

Not remaining in the vine has predictable consequences: "Abide in me as I abide in you. Just as the branch cannot bear fruit by itself unless it abides in the vine, neither can you unless you abide in me. . . . Those who abide in me and I in them bear much fruit, because apart from me you can do nothing" (John 15:4–5). Cut off from the vine, the branches might as well be thrown away. Apart from Christ, we can do nothing.

Living Reliance

As we seek to find out what we are to be doing with our lives in the world to fulfill the call of God, we discover that we are called to do nothing on our own. We require a living reliance upon Jesus Christ, the vine. He alone has done what we cannot do: He offered the perfect response of humanity to God.

This discovery, on the one hand, brings tremendous relief, for we are not expected to do what we are unable to do. We are not thrown back on ourselves and left to our own failings. Christ Jesus has lived the life of obedience on our behalf. He will fulfill in us now the life we were meant to live.

On the other hand, this discovery delivers a dire blow, a kind of death, for it signifies the end of pride and independence from God.

In an age of self-preoccupation, Christ calls us to living reliance and utter dependence. Of course, the secret lies in being connected to Jesus; in losing our self-will to him, we gain our whole lives. We become what we were meant to be, and we find fulfillment beyond measure. Our ability truly to choose and will what is good for us and for the world is restored. We thereby discover that we were meant not for isolated rugged independence but for communion with God and one another.

So the focus of life turns from self to Jesus Christ. We gaze upon his faithfulness. Here in the likeness of our own sinful flesh, he healed our humanity from within. For though tempted, he was obedient. Jesus lived in constant communication with the one he called "Abba." He embraced the broken ones and challenged the self-important ones. He remained faithful even to death on the cross. We concentrate then, not on ourselves and our inability, but on Jesus' life of obedience, which he offers to us.

Living reliance means our counting on what John Calvin called "the wonderful exchange." Jesus touched sinners like us and, far from being defiled, cleansed them. He touched the ill and, far from catching their disease, healed them. He welcomed the outcast and brought them within the fold of his care without condoning any sin or cruelly leaving people as they were. Rather, he restored them to the humanity they had lost. He embraced the world even unto death; and dying, far from being destroyed, he rose with eternal life for the world.

The one who prayed for us in the garden in his agony, prays for us even now at the right hand of God. He offers, as a human being, his worship on our behalf. He offers his obedience in our stead. He has become the Vine so that we might be branches. His life in us produces fruit. We do nothing but abide. He acts through us.

Lesslie Newbigin has written eloquently of this passage in his commentary on John, *The Light Has Come*: "This fruit is not an artifact of the disciples; it is the fruit of the vine. It is the life of Jesus himself reproduced in the lives of the disciples in the midst of the life of the world . . . the fruit is . . . love and obedience." [2]

On one hand, [God] demands our love and service and on the other, [God] is the actual source and originator of our ability to love and serve. We can only fully respond to the demand by fully accepting the gift; and to do this is the whole secret of the saints.

—Evelyn Underhill

Jesus' own love and obedience becomes ours as we are connected to the vine. The fruit of our lives is his humanity expressed through ours. We simply agree to stay connected. Newbigin continues,

> But it is necessary to "abide" in Jesus, and this means a continually renewed action of the will. It is the continually renewed decision that what has been done once for all by the action of Jesus shall be the basis, the starting point, the context of all my thinking and deciding and doing. . . . but "the loyalty demanded is not primarily a continual being *for*, but a being *from*; not the holding of a position but an allowing oneself to be held." (Bultmann)[3]

We consent to be in Jesus' care, to be where he has put us: restored, forgiven, included in his perfect humanity and obedience. We agree to be from him and to be held by him. We invite him to reproduce his life in us.

What are we supposed to do in the world for God? We begin by abiding in the vine. Moment by moment as life happens around us, we say, "Jesus, produce your life in me. I will go where you send me. I offer my life in your service to those around me—not because I am even able to be available to you but because you have grafted me into the vine. You produce fruit through me." Living reliance on the vine makes radical availability possible.

Let us focus on Jesus and on living reliance upon him. Professor Thomas F. Torrance has written,

> It is Christ the object of faith who holds on to us and saves us even when our faith is so weak. The Christ in whom we believe far exceeds the small measure of our faith, and so the believer finds . . . security not in [a] poor believing grasp of Christ but in the gift of grace. . . . It is not therefore upon the strength of our faith that we rely but upon the faithfulness of Christ.[4]

This reliance runs counter to our usual thinking. We chastise ourselves: I must do *more* for God. It seems impossible that doing nothing for God of our own will accomplishes far more. It feels as if we'll just be sitting around singing while the world dies. But as we begin to abide in the vine, inviting Jesus to produce his life in us and getting ourselves out of the way, our lives will become fruitful beyond imagination.

Jesus asks for radical availability, and we cannot offer it. He asks us if we love him more than anything; and we turn away our eyes, for we are full of self. He asks us to let go, and we walk away in shame, for we have many possessions. We can't do it.

But Jesus has already done it. He gave up all, as a mortal, for God. He loved God with all his heart, soul, mind, and body. He established the new vine. And he says, I did this for you. I am doing it for you. Will you agree to it? Will you let me do in you what you cannot? Will you let my faithfulness be the measure of your life? Will you let me hold you? Will you let me be life in you?

We blow off steam trying to control life rather than letting God's energy pass through us to enrich our lives and our world. We are so full of our own need to accomplish and to act that we have no room to receive the power God waits to bestow. If we approached life with open hands, in poverty of spirit, we could receive the resources we need for effective living. . . . Jesus did not make things happen. He allowed things to happen through him, through his openness and receptivity.

—Thomas R. Hawkins

DAILY EXERCISES

Read the chapter for Week 2, "Living Reliance." Keep a journal or blank book beside you to record your thoughts, questions, prayers, and images.

This week, use your daily exercise time to explore the meaning and promise of responding to God's call out of a "living reliance" on Christ. For example, as you seek to respond to God's calling, how are you encountering the limits of your self-reliance and hearing the invitation to a greater reliance on Christ? Remember the shift and promise contained in the words of the chapter:

> To share in the work of Christ, then, means not so much our working for Christ but our inviting him to work in and through us. . . . We grow toward that spiritual reality named by Paul in his Letter to the Galatians, "It is no longer I who live, but it is Christ who lives in me" (Gal. 2:20).

EXERCISE 1

Read John 15:1-5. Draw an image of a vine and its branches that illustrates what "living reliance" on Christ means to you. How would you interpret your image as a picture of the life you seek or the life that Christ seeks to live in you? (Draw on a sheet of paper, not in your journal. Bring your drawing to the group meeting where you may choose to display it on the center table for the opening worship. It need not be beautiful or artistic, simply expressive of the vine and branches.)

Bring to mind the primary activities that fill your life right now. In what ways do you feel that the activities of your life are connected or disconnected from the Lord? Spend the remainder of your time abiding in Christ and opening yourself to the flow of divine love in and through you.

EXERCISE 2

Read Acts 9:10-19. Ananias's vision of the Lord and the Lord's instructions concerning Saul remind us that the Lord sometimes nudges us to do things that we neither understand nor appreciate. Often we are tempted to discount or ignore such promptings. What inner nudging, dreams, or persistent thoughts seem to be urging you to reach out to certain persons or to act on certain concerns? What relationship do you sense between paying attention to these inner promptings and staying connected with Christ? Record your thoughts in your journal.

EXERCISE 3

Read Romans 7:14-25. Reflect on Paul's inner struggle and his deep frustration over his inability to live up to the expectations of God's law. Find places in your life where you identify with Paul's struggle and describe them in your own words. To what extent have these kinds of struggles brought you to greater reliance on Christ? What does it mean at these places of inner weakness to rely on Christ rather than on yourself to resolve the dilemma? In prayer, offer your weaknesses to Christ. Record what you experience and learn.

EXERCISE 4

Read 2 Corinthians 12:1-10. Paul's "thorn in the flesh" represents a weakness with which he struggled mightily, but precisely what it was remains a mystery. The significance comes in Paul's interpretation of it. He sees this thorn as God's way of deflating his inclination to boast so that God can work through him.

Meditate on Paul's living reliance, especially in the phrase, "My grace is sufficient for you, for power is made perfect in weakness." Is some aspect of who you are—some "thorn in the flesh" that will not go away—urging you to rely more on God in order to fulfill your calling? With what limitation do you struggle? What weakness embarrasses you? Perhaps God is calling you to see this thorn in a new way. In prayer, begin to make this area of weakness available to God and see what happens.

EXERCISE 5

Read 2 Corinthians 1:3-7. These verses remind us of another way we rely on God for the resources to respond to our call. God comforts

us in our affliction, Paul writes, so that we may be able to comfort others. Think of a past wound or hurt that has enabled you to feel compassion for persons who face similar challenges. What were the circumstances, and how did you experience God's consolation or call in the midst of your affliction (v. 3)? How is God calling you to use your suffering for the sake of others? In prayer, begin to offer your wounds to the God who heals and redeems.

Remember to review your journal for the week in preparation for the group meeting.

Part 4, Week 3
Bearing the Fruit of the Vine

*D*o you feel as if we have been bouncing back and forth between extremes? The question has been, "What am I supposed to be doing for God?" The answers have seemed contradictory: everything and nothing. God lays claim to everything, absolutely every corner and crevice of our beings. Yet at the same time, we realize that we can do nothing on our own. Apart from Christ Jesus, "our striving would be losing" as Martin Luther said.

So what are we supposed to be doing? Answers to the question that are just slightly off the mark can send us barreling down terribly defeating paths. If we try too hard to be constantly available, we may end up becoming Christian perfectionists. We may hate ourselves for our failures. We may start trying to do more (and trying to get everyone else to do more), always striving to measure up to what God requires and never making it. We may become mean, legalistic, guilt-slinging Christians. On the other hand, we may become so enamored of grace, counting on God to do everything, that we get lazy. We may wait so passively for God to work through us that we end up with no prayer life, no service life, no discipline, and no hope. In such a state, we can hardly be distinguished from much of the culture.

The balance lies in the image of the branch remaining in the vine that we began considering last week. We look at a vine or a tree and

How do we discover which part of God's vision is ours? Insight comes when we reflect on what evokes our most passionate criticism, our deepest grief, or energizes us to new possibilities. . . . When we pay attention . . . we begin to get glimmers of the aspects of God's vision that may be ours to carry out.

—Jacqueline McMakin
with Rhoda Nary

rarely give a second thought as to how the branches remain connected to the larger trunk. A branch is held by the tree even as the branch holds to the tree. The bark joins the two so that we cannot really tell where one begins and the other ends. The branch is a conduit for the vine and receives water and nutrients from its trunk. In this way the tree or vine grows up through its branches. And those branches produce fruit according to their design.

No branch lives without connection to the source. It does not try to leap off and become an independent tree. Neither does it resist the design of the vine, trying to block its natural growth. A branch on a grapevine allows grapes to come forth without effort.

When we translate this image to the relationship between Christ and us, we readily see that we are called to dwell in him. We do not try to live apart from Jesus Christ. We consent to be in the position he has given us. He has declared us to be branches in him, the Vine. Our position is a result of the work he has done.

The fruit we produce will be Jesus' life coming forth through us. This consideration of what we are to do in the world continually returns to who Jesus is, what he has done and is doing in the world.

The Fruit of Love

Lesslie Newbigin notes that in Jesus' life on earth, he did not enter each day with a fixed agenda or an inflexible, planned course. Rather, he lived to be interrupted. The changing, unexpected occurrences of daily life produced the opportunities for love. Jesus expressed his love for God through availability to love whoever came before him in whatever way was required. He obeyed the demands of such love for the world even to the point of dying a criminal's death upon the cross as an innocent man:

> Jesus had no program of his own. He planned no career for himself. . . . He simply responded in loving obedience to the will of his Father as it was presented to him in all the accidents, contingencies, and interruptions of daily life, among all the personal and public ambitions and fears and jealousies of that little province of the Roman empire.[1]

Jesus' life provides the pattern for us. Dwelling in his great love, held in his grace even as the vine holds the branches, we welcome the reproduction of such love through us. Jesus told his disciples, "As the Father has loved me, so I have loved you; abide in my love. If you keep my commandments, you will abide in my love, just as I have kept my Father's commandments and abide in his love . . . love one another as I have loved you" (John 15:9-10, 12). Being companions in Christ means loving in the way Jesus did. Newbigin continues,

> So the disciple. . . . will not be concerned to create a character or career for himself. He will leave that to the wise husbandry of the Gardener who alone knows what pruning, what watering and feeding, what sunshine or rain, warmth or cold is needed to produce the fruit he desires. The disciple will "learn obedience" by following Jesus in the same kind of moment-by-moment obedience to the will of the Father as it is disclosed in the contingent happenings of daily life in the place and time where God has put him.[2]

The measure of our lives will not be in career and the name or place we make for ourselves. These things may come. But the deeper measure is the love and obedience we show in the midst of life that sometimes sends us rising to the stars and other times sends us crashing to the depths. We honor God in our daily tasks and work. But even more important than what we do is how we do it. Is the legacy of my labor one of love? Can I see an interruption as a call of God? Do I understand that my life is not really my work or status or success but my life in Christ Jesus expressing itself in love for those around me?

The Apostle Paul summarized all we have been considering: "The only thing that counts is faith working through love" (Gal. 5:6). What matters in life is the faith by which we say yes to Christ Jesus and the way we express such faith toward others in love. That's the essence of our Christian call, whether we are functioning at full capacity in an extremely demanding job or lying paralyzed from the neck down on a hospital bed. Whether we are overextended in a plethora of relationships or lonely from leave-takings, the call of God is the same: faith expressing itself through love. Faith takes the position of receiving grace in Christ Jesus. Love enacts that grace toward others.

The bonds that connect us are the bonds of love, God's love for us, which draws us, but also our love for God and neighbor, which can never be separated from each other. . . . We cannot love God and hate or even be indifferent to our neighbor.

—Roberta C. Bondi

The Role of the Holy Spirit

What is required of us is quite simple. Yet the balance of radical availability, living reliance, and fruitful love is hard to maintain. We keep getting in the way of what God in Christ wants to do through us. The reality of sin defeats our impulse toward love with old grudges, present lusts, or anxieties about the future. Abiding in Christ is supposed to be as effortless as being branches on the tree, but our lives reveal that it is not that easy.

At this point we must recall the person of God the Holy Spirit. Shortly before his crucifixion, Jesus promised his disciples that though he would be leaving them, he would send the Holy Spirit to dwell within and among them. The Spirit would bring to mind the words of Jesus and teach the disciples the true meaning of his life, death, and resurrection. Jesus said that it is the work of the Spirit to take what is of Jesus—his faithfulness, his love, his obedience, his forgiveness—and give it to us (John 16:14-15). So the presence of the Holy Spirit within us is the key to our continual abiding in Christ Jesus, which leads to a fruitful life.

Paul tells us that "God's love has been poured into our hearts through the Holy Spirit that has been given to us" (Rom. 5:5). By that Spirit, we are adopted in Christ as God's sons and daughters. Therefore, when we cry out to God in prayer, "it is that very Spirit bearing witness with our spirit that we are children of God" (Rom. 8:16). The Holy Spirit is God consenting to live within us, ever urging us from the inside out toward a deeper relationship with Christ. Here is the source of our believing and our acting. Paul states, "Through the Spirit, by faith, we eagerly wait for the hope of righteousness" (Gal. 5:5), which Jesus has accomplished for us.

And the Spirit is the source of power for winning the struggle against the old nature and sustaining growth even amidst difficult circumstances. Paul prays that his readers will "be strengthened in [their] inner being with power through [God's] Spirit" (Eph. 3:16). This mighty strength enables us to deny sin and live for God. By the Spirit, we "put to death the deeds" (Rom. 8:13) of the sinful self and live vigorously for God.

Andrew Murray has written eloquently of the role of the Holy Spirit in connecting us to Christ: "All the fulness is in Jesus; the fulness of grace and truth, out of which we receive grace for grace. The Holy Spirit is the appointed conveyancer, whose special work it is to make Jesus and all there is in Him for us ours in personal appropriation, in blessed experience. He is the Spirit of life in Christ Jesus."[3]

The Spirit is the conveyer of Jesus Christ and all his graces to us and through us. Abiding in Christ then is the work of the Holy Spirit within us. By the creative, life-giving power of God the Spirit, fruit is grown though us.

Our part, though small, is crucial. We are to ask the Spirit to work in us and to consent consciously and deliberately to being branches in the vine that is Jesus Christ. Each moment requires such openness of us. We renew our consent to let the Spirit flow through us day by day and hour by hour. Murray continues, "Just as the branch, already filled with the sap of the vine, is ever crying for the continued and increasing flow of that sap, that it may bring its fruit to perfection, so the believer, rejoicing in the possession of the Spirit, ever thirsts and cries for more."[4]

We may thus pray continually, "God, I cannot. But you can. By your grace I am connected to Jesus Christ. I agree to what you have done! And I know that even my agreeing is a gift. Nevertheless, you desire this act of my will. So by the power of the Holy Spirit, whom you have caused to dwell in me, grow the fruit of love in my daily life."

The scriptures employ many images for this action of living reliance that leads to the fruit of the vine. The archetypal example is Mary's response to Gabriel, when the angel announces that she will conceive the Son of God. She replies, "Here I am, the servant of the Lord; let it be with me according to your word" (Luke 1:38). Gabriel has revealed what God will do. Mary does not have to create the plan or muster the power of God. She simply agrees. Based on a devoted, loving relationship as the servant and handmaiden of God, she invites God to go ahead and act in accordance with the promise made. This kind of active consent to what God desires to do in and through us is the way to become fruitful branches of the Vine. We do not try to

As the union of the branch with the vine is one of growth, never-ceasing growth and increase, so our abiding in Christ is a life process in which the divine life takes ever fuller and more complete possession of us.

—Andrew Murray

manufacture the fruit in our own strength; we actively choose to invite God to grow the fruit through us.

Fruit and Gifts

Fruit is expected of every Christian, regardless of stage or condition of life. In John 15, Jesus defined this fruit in terms of love and obedience. Paul expanded the image when he wrote, "The fruit of the Spirit is love, joy, peace, patience, kindness, generosity, faithfulness, gentleness, and self-control" (Gal. 5:22-23). These attitudes and actions characterize the life lived in obedience to God and reliance on the Holy Spirit. We cannot make ourselves produce such fruit. But we can ask God to grow such love through us. And we can focus our minds toward exhibiting such qualities.

To use another scriptural image for this process, we dress ourselves in the clothing of the Spirit (Col. 3:12-17). This is not done in the sense of covering up our true nature with the appearance of Christian values. Rather, based on our identity in Christ, we consciously adorn ourselves with the clothes appropriate to our position. Since we are branches in the vine that is Christ Jesus, we may deliberately cultivate what suits our station in life. We want to look the part that has been given to us. Again without trying to do it in our own strength, we set our imaginations, focus our minds, and direct our actions in accord with what Christ Jesus has said he wants to do in us.

With this necessary foundation laid, we may begin to consider what specific work in the world God wants to do through us. We may now ponder how God has given each of us a particular gift for service that makes our place in the whole vineyard splendidly unique. Every Christian has been so gifted for service that the universal church of Christ renders a marvelous diversity of ministry within the unity of the Spirit. Fruit takes precedence over gifts. But the gifts give zest to our living reliance and continual obedience. In the next section, we will consider more closely the nature of spiritual gifts and their place as we join in the work of Christ.

There is simply no way we can be obedient to the command to love without grafting ourselves onto the vine of Christ: "Whoever remains in me, with me in him, / bears fruit in plenty; / for cut off from me you can do nothing"(John 15:5). The choice set before us is therefore the choice of enlargement or withering.

—Robin Maas

DAILY EXERCISES

Read the chapter for Week 3, "Bearing the Fruit of the Vine," before you begin the exercises. Keep your journal beside you to record your thoughts, questions, prayers, and insights.

This week use your daily exercise time to explore the fruitfulness of your response to God's call, not in terms of how much you are doing but in terms of who you are becoming through the spirit of Jesus Christ. Drawing on Jesus' image of the vine and branches in John 15, think about whether there have been any new buds of life in you in the past few weeks, or during your participation in *Companions in Christ* thus far. What fruit is the Vine already producing in and through you?

EXERCISE 1

Read Romans 1:7. Meditate on what it means that you are "God's beloved . . . , who are called to be saints." List three to five persons, living or dead, who embody this meaning for you. Do not include biblical characters. Under each name, note the qualities of humanness and holiness that draw you to that person, and why. Pray with the affirmation, "We are God's beloved . . . , who are called to be saints."

EXERCISE 2

Read Galatians 5:13-26. Meditate on the fruit of the Spirit listed and on evidence of the fruit in your life in community. What do you see? What fruit would others say they see in you?

Identify an area of your life where you feel you are not bearing the fruit of the Spirit. What would it mean for you to let yourself be guided by the Spirit who already lives in you? Spend some time in prayer asking the Spirit to help you with these challenges. Jot down any insights that may come.

EXERCISE 3

Read Philippians 3:2-11. Paul uses strong words to warn the Philippians of the temptation among religious people to mistake adherence

to a set of religious practices or conformity to a moral code for the fruit of life in Christ. How do you distinguish between the two in your life—your own efforts to create a good life and the fruit that comes from abiding in Christ?

Draw a circle. Around the boundary, write all of the commitments and efforts you make to live a good life, including achievements that make you proud. Within the circle, write words or images that represent the full fruit of life in Christ for which you long. Reflect on the relationship you see between what is around and what is within the circle. In prayer, open your heart to the goodness God gives us through faith in Christ.

EXERCISE 4

Read Acts 2:42-47. Reflect on the close relationship between the abundant fruit of the early church and the root practices of that community. Make a list (or draw a picture) of the fruits and roots that you see in the description.

Now turn your attention to your congregation. What fruit do you experience in your church? What fruit does the surrounding community see and experience? What are the root practices of your congregation that nourish those fruits? In prayer, ask God to show you the underlying condition of your spiritual roots as a church. Note your responses.

EXERCISE 5

Read Romans 8:18-28. Where in your community are creation's inhabitants "subjected to futility" and yearning to be set free from "bondage to decay"? Pray for renewal there, offering yourself to the renewing influence of the Spirit in those places. Record your thoughts and experience.

Review your journal for the week in preparation for the group meeting.

Part 4, Week 4
Gifts of the Spirit

*W*e have been considering what God wants us to do in the world. We know that God asks for our complete availability, and we know that apart from the grace of Jesus Christ, we can do nothing. On our own, we are unable even to believe in God's love or offer our lives in service. But by the power of the Holy Spirit, we may live for God. Abiding in Christ as branches remain in the vine, we give our consent for God to produce fruit through us. That fruit includes love, joy, peace, patience, kindness, goodness—the very life of Christ Jesus reproduced through us.

The fruit of the Spirit may grow in the dullest, slowest, and weakest, as well as in the brightest, fastest, and strongest. Astonishingly, God chooses to work through available vessels, no matter how broken or worn we seem to be, in whatever circumstances we happen to be. Royalty and servants, bosses and workers, able-bodied and infirm—all have one basic vocation. All are called to consent to the work of Christ in their life; all are called to show the love of Jesus to others by the same Spirit.

Our common grace and task being clear, we may now celebrate the wonderful variety in God's creative work. Every Christian has been given a spiritual gift. Simply defined, spiritual gifts are particular abilities given by Christ through the Holy Spirit for the good of the whole church so it may do Christ's work in the world.

There are many different gifts. Scholars list anywhere from a minimum of nineteen up to thirty-one, with some saying there is no end to the variety of gifts God bestows. Each one of us has at least one spiritual gift that complements our God-given personality and character. Our gift or gifts cry out for expression and use. And using our gifts brings a great release of energy coupled with joy. We feel as if we are doing easily just what we have always wanted to do.

Over the next two weeks, you will have the opportunity to help others in your group discern their particular gifts, while allowing them to help you discern your own. How you may develop and use these gifts in Christ's service will be a matter of continuing discernment. This reading prepares you for that work as we consider the basic scriptural texts on spiritual gifts.

The Holy Spirit, Giver of All Gifts

Paul begins, "Now concerning spiritual gifts, brothers and sisters, I do not want you to be uninformed" (1 Cor. 12:1). Right away, we may realize that spiritual gifts can cause confusion in a church, and their healthy use requires accurate knowledge about these gifts. Before going further, Paul sets spiritual gifts in their context. He reminds his readers of the foundational importance of the Holy Spirit: "No one can say 'Jesus is Lord' except by the Holy Spirit" (1 Cor. 12:3). Paul credits our most basic confession to God the Holy Spirit. Here we may take his cue and consider the Spirit more deeply before proceeding.

The great Swiss Reformer, John Calvin, writes convincingly of our need for the Spirit's work:

> First, we must understand that as long as Christ remains outside of us, and we are separated from him, all that he has suffered and done for the salvation of the human race remains useless and of no value to us. . . . It is true that we obtain this by faith. . . .
>
> But faith is the principal work of the Holy Spirit. [It is] a supernatural gift that those who would otherwise remain in unbelief receive Christ by faith. . . .
>
> [Christ] unites himself to us by the Spirit alone. By the grace and power of the same Spirit we are made his members. . . . To sum up, the Holy Spirit is the bond by which Christ effectually unites us to himself.[1]

Beloved young Christian, take time to understand and to become filled with the truth: the Holy Spirit is in you. Review all the assurances of God's word that this is so. . . . Pray, think not for a moment of living as a Christian without the indwelling of the Spirit. Take pains to have your heart filled with the faith that the Spirit dwells in you, and will do . . . mighty work, for through faith the Spirit comes and works.

—Andrew Murray

46

God the Holy Spirit creates faith in us so that we may see and believe who Jesus is. Then the Spirit unites all the love and obedience of Jesus Christ to us. The bond or spiritual glue of the Spirit joins us to Christ. On our own, all the love of Jesus is outside us. By the Spirit's uniting, knitting, and weaving, Jesus comes to dwell within us.

This work is the very power of God, but it is not violent to creatures as fragile as we. The Spirit, in divine humility, works gently with us, inviting our cooperation and enduring patiently our storms of willfulness. Professor Thomas F. Torrance writes, "If it is only the Almighty who can be infinitely gentle, the Holy Spirit may well be characterized as the gentleness of God the Father Almighty."[2] The Spirit woos rather than overwhelms and whispers more than shouts. Torrance quotes the ancient writings of Cyril: "His coming is gentle. Our perception of him is fragrant; his burden is very easy to bear; beams of light shine out with his coming. He comes with the compassion of a true Guardian, for he comes to save and to heal, to teach, to admonish, to strengthen, to exhort, to enlighten the mind."[3]

As light falls upon the world silently, invisibly, doing its work of sustaining all life, so the Spirit falls upon us and shines within us in a quiet, steady way. All the while, the Holy Spirit humbly illumines Jesus Christ, giving him the glory and prominence and directing our attention to rely upon him alone.

While bringing the gift of faith, the Spirit also labors to make us more and more like Jesus. Calvin writes, "By his secret watering, the Spirit makes us fruitful to bring forth the bud of righteousness. . . . For by the inspiration of his power he so breathes divine life into us that we are no longer actuated by ourselves, but are ruled by his action and prompting."[4]

The Holy Spirit, though gentle, does work in power, "persistently boiling away and burning up our vicious and inordinate desires, he enflames our hearts with the love of God." In summary, Calvin tells us that "whatever good things are in us are the fruits of [the Spirit's] grace."[5] This is the sweet, mighty Spirit at work in the church who, in addition to faith and fruit, bestows gifts upon us.

Have a great reverence for the work of the Spirit in you. Seek [the Spirit] every day to believe, to obey, to trust, and [the Spirit] will take and make known to you all that there is in Jesus. [The Holy Spirit] will make Jesus very glorious to you and in you.

—Andrew Murray

From this foundation, Paul can say that the same Spirit who enables a similar basic faith in every Christian also dispenses a wide variety of spiritual gifts. Each one of us is "given the manifestation of the Spirit" (1 Cor. 12:7). In other words, the spirit of Jesus Christ is made known through believers in wonderfully diverse ways. Every believer is different, yet each one is gifted. No one is passed over. God delights to give gifts to us since we are dearly loved children. And God is infinite in creativity, so we do not all come out exactly the same. God rejoices in the variety.

The grace of God in Christ Jesus is poured out like a great wave over the church. But that metaphor goes only so far. The wave of God's grace does not wash everything into a bland sameness. Rather, grace polishes each one to a unique brilliance. None is expendable. We are not better when some are absent. The church is at its best with all present and the unique combinations of gifts flourishing.

Every single one of us has been made to shine. There is a particular gift in you. You have a part to play that no one else can. You add a nuance to the story of God's love in Christ that makes it more wonderful. You add a color to the palate of grace. Without your gift the hues are not as vivid. As Paul says, all the gifts "are activated by one and the same Spirit, who allots to each one individually just as the Spirit chooses" (1 Cor. 12:11).

These individually tailored gifts, however, are not only for our personal enjoyment. Paul finishes the sentence, "To each is given the manifestation of the Spirit for the common good." Here we may switch from the image of the vine and its branches to the image of the body of Christ: "For just as the body is one and has many members, and all the members of the body, though many, are one body, so it is with Christ. For in the one Spirit, we were all baptized into one body. . . . Now you are the body of Christ and individually members of it" (1 Cor. 12:12-13, 27). Paul describes how all the parts of the body must work together in order for the whole to function. Next week we will consider more closely the different expressions of the body of Christ manifested in various churches, and how, like bodies, each has

The gifts [of the Spirit] are a means of transmitting the powerful and purposeful divine presence into the flesh and blood of humanity. It is an intimacy with God that sheds light on the active presence of the resurrected Christ. It is an inner power that makes the whole person receptive and obedient to a new way of living abundantly and effectively in service to God's kingdom.

—Charles V. Bryant

a particular shape, character, and temperament. For now, we realize that the gifts are meant to benefit the whole.

First Corinthians 12 names gifts that may seem splashier than other lists in the New Testament: working of miracles, discernment of spirits, various kinds of tongues, interpretation of those tongues, gifts of healing. With these are included gifts more readily under-stood, such as faith, wisdom, forms of assistance, and leadership. We realize that the Spirit comes to us in power, and the community of Christ's people may expect to see many wondrous sights. Yet these more demonstrative gifts are to be balanced with wise and discerning minds.

Gifts That Unify the Body

In Ephesians 4:1-16, Paul concentrates on the importance of our unity as one body of Jesus Christ. The gifts discussion is again placed in its context. Paul begins by reminding us of our most basic calling to follow Jesus and urges us "to lead a life worthy of the calling to which you have been called" (v. 1). The common expression of our call is the fruit of the Spirit, here described as living "with all humil-ity and gentleness, with patience, bearing with one another in love, making every effort to maintain the unity of the Spirit in the bond of peace" (vv. 2-3).

Then Paul goes on to describe our common foundation of "one Lord, one faith, one baptism, one God and Father of all" (vv. 5-6). From that shared core, God's diversity arises: "But each of us was given grace according to the measure of Christ's gift" (v. 7). Jesus who dwelt among us also ascended to heaven, and from his place at the right hand of God he poured forth the Holy Spirit onto the disciples. With the Spirit come gifts: "The gifts he gave were that some would be apostles, some prophets, some evangelists, some pastors and teach-ers, to equip the saints for the work of ministry, for building up the body of Christ, until all of us come to the unity of the faith and of the knowledge of the Son of God, to maturity, to the measure of the full stature of Christ" (vv. 11-13).

The gifts listed in Ephesians are for leadership. Gifted leaders equip the rest of the believers, the saints, for the ministry of the whole church. Leadership builds up the body so that as one, we grow to be more and more like Christ. Joining in the work of Christ means becoming like him, and that forming process occurs through the exercise of spiritual gifts. The apostles were eyewitnesses to the resurrected Jesus and laid the foundation for the church through the ages by bearing witness to all that Jesus said and did. Prophets build on that base, calling the church out from the world to be a people dedicated first to God. Evangelists can then lead the church back into the world with the message of the gospel. Pastors nurture members of the body through the stresses of life, while teachers continually link daily living with the stories and truths of scripture. Together, such leadership equips a body that both gathers together and is sent into the world. The gifts employed make the body healthy and strong as it expresses the work of Christ.

One Body, Gifted for Service

Romans 12:1-8 focuses on less spectacular gifts that are no less important than the apparent gifts in First Corinthians or the strong leadership gifts in Ephesians. As ever, Paul sets the context before speaking of the gifts themselves. Here he urges his readers toward radical availability. His appeal is based, however, not on an individual's effort to please God but on the mercies first given by God in Christ. Realizing these, we may present our bodies "as a living sacrifice." Such consecration is continual, and its fruit is being "transformed by the renewing of your minds." This is an organic change, created by God but consented to and chosen by us day by day.

From here, Paul employs the image of the body to express how each of us is important yet all of us are interrelated: "For as in one body we have many members, and not all the members have the same function, so we, who are many, are one body in Christ, and individually we are members one of another" (vv. 4-5). The organically connected communion of believers is yet individually gifted for service to one another: "We have gifts that differ according to the grace given to us" (v. 6). Paul encourages believers to act in love in accordance with our unique gifts, to use who we are and what we have, not trying to be anyone else but vigorously being who God has made us to be: "prophecy, in proportion to faith; ministry, in ministering; the teacher, in teaching; the exhorter, in exhortation; the giver, in generosity; the leader, in diligence; the compassionate, in cheerfulness" (vv. 6-8).

This passage echoes Ecclesiastes 9:10: "Whatever your hand finds to do, do with your might." We are called to kindle the gifts by using them in service. The more we employ our gifts, the more they blossom. By contrast, stifling or hiding our gifts can lead to spiritual diminishment.

So, what are your gifts, and what are the gifts of those with whom you have been traveling as companions in Christ these past several weeks or months? Where are you and your group friends already using your gifts? Where do you feel led to be using them? The exercises this week and your meeting time will help you discern your unique spiritual gifts and those of your companions.

We develop our gifts . . . when we use them for the good of others. . . . Our gifts are to be given away so that the whole human community is richer for our having been here.

—Joan D. Chittister

DAILY EXERCISES

Read the chapter for Week 4, "Gifts of the Spirit." Keep a journal or blank book beside you to record your thoughts and insights.

Your primary assignment for each daily exercise time is to begin to name the gifts that you have observed in each person in your small group. You will be given some scripture for reflection but direct the majority of your time toward this preparing for the group meeting. Each day select one to three group members for prayer and naming of gifts. Focus on one person at a time, and ask God for an awareness to see and celebrate the gifts God has given him or her.

- First, think about each person's unique contribution as a group member since the beginning of your time together.
- Second, recall what he or she has communicated during the past three sessions about the things most enjoyed, the dreams for a better world, and the potentials for love latent in wounds and weaknesses.
- Then record your insights and affirmations in your journal.

When you have gathered your affirmations and insights about a person, read over the list of New Testament gifts printed at the end of the exercises for this week (pages 217–21), and search for gifts you associate with what you have seen. Interpret the gifts broadly and creatively. Although you should not feel overly constrained by the list (there are other gifts), try to stay within the list as far as you are able before you name others.

Finally, write a card to each group member identifying and affirming gifts. In the cards you will describe

1. Gifts you clearly see in each person. Beside or beneath each gift, add a few words describing how and where you have seen these gifts.
2. Gifts you see as potentials in each person. Describe briefly how or where you have seen these potentials.

Important: Before the meeting, compare your cards to a group roster to make sure you have cards for everyone. Your group leader will inform you if this process will require one or two meetings (depending on the size of your group) and which members will wait until the second meeting to receive their cards if two meetings are needed. Bring the cards to the next group meeting.

EXERCISE 1

Read Ephesians 4:7-13. Meditate on the hope of growing together "to maturity, to the measure of the full stature of Christ." Think about that in light of this week's work of affirming one another's gifts for Christ's ministry. Follow the guidelines for completing gift cards, and begin the process of writing a card for each group member.

Consider what it would mean for these persons to grow to maturity according to the measure of the full stature of Christ. Pray for their maturity in using the gifts God has given them. Pray for your ability to speak the truth in love concerning their gifts so that they may see their gifts with new clarity.

EXERCISE 2

Read 1 Corinthians 12:1-27. Meditate on the mystery of our relationship in Christ and our dependence on one another for building up the full ministry of Christ. Follow the guidelines for completing a gift card for each group member.

Use any remaining time to reflect on your own gifts. Draw an image of a physical body. Figuratively speaking, where would you locate yourself and your gifts if this were a picture of the body of Christ in your congregation? Name the gifts that are implied by locating yourself there.

EXERCISE 3

Read Matthew 25:14-30. Meditate on the good news that God has given gifts to each group member for the increase of God's kingdom on earth. Offer a prayer that each may discover his or her gifts and use

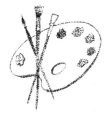

them well rather than bury or hide them. Follow the guidelines for completing a gift card for each group member.

Use any remaining time to reflect on the two kinds of persons Jesus describes in the parable of the talents. In what ways do you see yourself in both characters?

EXERCISE 4

Read Romans 12:1-8. Meditate on Paul's counsel that we think about our gifts with "sober judgment, each according to the measure of faith that God has assigned." Follow the guidelines for completing a gift card for each member of the group.

Use any remaining time to identify attitudes that limit your ability to appreciate others' gifts or to value your own gifts. Offer these attitudes to God in all honesty. Ask God to free you to appreciate your friends the way you want them to appreciate you.

EXERCISE 5

Read 2 Timothy 1:2-7. Ponder the powerful and confirming role that we play in recognizing and naming one another's gifts. Follow the guidelines for completing a gift card for each group member.

Use any remaining time to reflect on persons who have kindled "the gift of God" in you and called forth your gifts. What qualities in them helped you to be yourself? Pray for the grace to be such a faithful friend for the members of your group.

Please review your journal entries for the week in preparation for the group meeting.

A List of Spiritual Gifts

Dan R. Dick wrote the following list; it is used by permission. (See footnote on page 59.)

These gifts are derived from Paul's listings of spiritual gifts in Romans 12:6-8; 1 Corinthians 12:4-11; 12:27-31; Ephesians 4:11-12.

Administration—The gift of organizing human and material resources for the work of Christ, including the ability to plan and work with people to delegate responsibilities, track progress, and evaluate the effectiveness of procedures. Administrators attend to details, communicate effectively, and take as much pleasure in working behind the scenes as they do in standing in the spotlight.

Apostleship—The gift of spreading the gospel of Jesus Christ to other cultures and foreign lands. This is the missionary zeal that moves us from the familiar into uncharted territory to share the good news. Apostles embrace opportunities to learn foreign languages, visit other cultures, and go where people are who have not heard the Christian message. . . . It is no longer necessary to cross an ocean to enter the mission field. Even across generations, we may find that we need to "speak other languages" just to communicate. Our mission field might be no further than our own backyard.

Compassion—This gift is exceptional empathy with those in need that moves us to action. More than just concern, compassion demands that we share the suffering of others in order to connect the gospel truth with other realities of life. Compassion moves us beyond our comfort zones to offer practical, tangible aid to all God's children, regardless of the worthiness of the recipients or the response we receive for our service.

Discernment—This is the ability to separate truth from erroneous teachings and to rely on spiritual intuition to know what God is calling us to do. Discernment allows us to focus on what is truly important and to ignore that which deflects us from faithful obedience to

God. Discernment aids us in knowing whom to listen to and whom to avoid.

Evangelism—This is the ability to share the gospel of Jesus Christ with those who have not heard it before or with those who have not yet made a decision for Christ. This gift is manifested in both one-on-one situations and in group settings, both large and small. It is an intimate relationship with another person or persons that requires the sharing of personal faith and a call for a response of faith to God.

Exhortation—This is the gift of exceptional encouragement. Exhorters see the silver lining in every cloud, offer deep and inspiring hope to the fellowship, and look for and commend the best in everyone. Exhorters empower the community of faith to feel good about itself and to feel hopeful for the future. Exhorters are not concerned by appearances; they hold fast to what they know to be true and right and good.

Faith—More than just belief, faith is a gift that empowers an individual or a group to hold fast to its identity in Christ in the face of any challenge. The gift of faith enables believers to rise above pressures and problems that might otherwise cripple them. Faith is characterized by an unshakable trust in God to deliver on God's promises, no matter what. The gift of faith inspires those who might be tempted to give up to hold on.

Giving—Beyond the regular response of gratitude to God that all believers make, giving as a gift is the ability to use the resource of money to support the work of the body of Christ. Giving is the ability to manage money to the honor and glory of God. Givers can discern the best ways to put money to work, can understand the validity and practicality of appeals for funds, and can guide [church leaders] in the most faithful methods for managing [the congregation's] financial concerns.

Healing—This is the gift of channeling God's healing powers into the lives of God's people. Physical, emotional, spiritual, and psychological healing are all ways that healers manifest this gift. Healers are prayerful, and they help people understand that healing is in the hands of God, that healing is often more than just erasing negative symptoms. Some of the most powerful healers display some of the most heartbreaking afflictions.

Helping—This is the gift of making sure that everything is ready for the work of Christ to occur. Helpers assist others to accomplish the mission and ministry of the church. These "unsung heroes" work behind the scenes and attend to details that others would rather not be bothered with. Helpers function faithfully, regardless of the credit or attention they receive. Helpers provide the framework upon which the ministry of the church is built.

Interpretation of Tongues (see Tongues)—This gift has two very different understandings: (1) the ability to interpret *foreign languages* without the necessity of formal study to communicate with those who have not heard the Christian message or (2) the ability to interpret the gift of tongues as a *secret prayer language* that communicates with God at a deep spiritual level. Both understandings are communal in nature: the first extends the good news into the world; the second strengthens the faith within the fellowship.

Knowledge—This is the gift of knowing the truth through faithful study of the Scripture and the human situation. Knowledge provides the information necessary for the transformation of the world and formation of the body of Christ. Those possessing this gift challenge the fellowship to improve itself through study, reading of the Scripture, discussions, and prayer.

Leadership—This is the gift of orchestrating the gifts and resources of others to achieve the mission and ministry of the church. Leaders move the community of faith toward a God-given vision of service, and they enable others to use their gifts to the very best of their abilities. Leaders are capable of creating synergy, whereby the community of faith accomplishes much more than its individual members could achieve on their own.

Miracle working—This gift enables the church to operate at a spiritual level that recognizes the miraculous work of God in the world. Miracle workers invoke God's power to accomplish that which appears impossible by worldly standards. Miracle workers remind the fellowship of the extraordinary nature of the ordinary world, thereby increasing faithfulness and trust in God. Miracle workers pray for God to work in the lives of others, and they feel no sense of surprise when their prayers are answered.

Prophecy—This is the gift of speaking the Word of God clearly and faithfully. Prophets allow God to speak through them to communicate the message that people most need to hear. While often unpopular, prophets are able to say what needs to be said because of the spiritual empowerment they receive. Prophets do not foretell the future, but proclaim God's future by revealing God's perspective on our current reality.

Servanthood—This is the gift of serving the spiritual and material needs of other people. . . . Servants understand their place in the body of Christ as giving comfort and aid to all who are in need. Servants look to the needs of others rather than focus on their own needs. To serve is to put faith into action; it is to treat others as if they were indeed Jesus Christ himself. The gift of service extends our Christian love into the world.

Shepherding—This is the gift of guidance. Shepherds nurture other Christians in the faith and provide a mentoring relationship to those who are new to the faith. Displaying an unusual spiritual maturity, shepherds share from their experience and learning to facilitate the spiritual growth and development of others. Shepherds take individuals under their care and walk with them on their spiritual journeys. Many shepherds provide spiritual direction and guidance to a wide variety of believers.

Teaching—This is the gift of bringing scriptural and spiritual truths to others. More than just teaching church school, teachers witness to the truth of Jesus Christ in a variety of ways, and they help others to understand the complex realities of the Christian faith. Teachers are revealers. They shine the light of understanding into the darkness of doubt and ignorance. They open people to new truths, and they challenge people to be more in the future than they have been in the past.

Tongues (see Interpretation of Tongues)—This gift has two popular interpretations: (1) the ability to communicate the gospel to other people in a *foreign language* without the benefit of having studied said language (see Acts 2:4) or (2) the ability to speak to God in a secret, unknown *prayer language* that can only be understood by a person possessing the gift of interpretation. The gift of speaking in the language of another culture makes the gift of tongues valuable for spreading the gospel throughout the world, while the gift of speaking a secret prayer language offers the opportunity to build faithfulness within a community of faith.

Wisdom—This is the gift of translating life experience into spiritual truth and of seeing the application of scriptural truth to daily living. The wise in our fellowships offer balance and understanding that transcend reason. Wisdom applies a God-given common sense to our understanding of God's plan for the church. Wisdom helps the community of faith remain focused on the important work of the church, and it enables younger, less mature Christians to benefit from those who have been blessed by God to share deep truths.

From *Revolutionizing Christian Stewardship for the 21st Century: Lessons from Copernicus* by Dan R. Dick (Nashville, Tenn.: Discipleship Resources, 1997), 97–101. Used by permission.

The Body of Christ Given for the World

The Holy Spirit has poured out gifts for service upon every believer. When we employ our gifts in the church, we discover a marvelous sense of energy and fulfillment. The gifts are meant to draw us ever more deeply into community with the other members of Christ's body. And that body is meant to grow: Our arms are continually open to welcome new members with their unique gifts. A living body maintains a steady state and shape, yet is simultaneously always changing and constantly replenishing itself. So the church remains always centered on Jesus Christ but is nevertheless not static but dynamic, not closed but open in its communion. Through the healthy use of spiritual gifts, the church grows and adapts in ever new ways, even while maintaining its basic form as the body of Christ.

Our spiritual gifts are not necessarily connected to our talents or education or what we do for a living. Our place in the body of Christ may differ greatly from our place in the workaday world. Thus in the church we may have a new identity. In the church, world leaders may become recipients and humble servers, while the meek of the world may become celebrated leaders. The CEO who bears so many expectations at work is free in the body of Christ to get on the floor and cuddle children in the nursery. A homemaking mother who converses with children all week may be a wise elder in the body of Christ. The

church of Jesus Christ grounds us in a life more real than the daily world and provides us with a deep sense of purpose and belonging.

Sending and Gathering

When Jesus first drew his followers together, he did not turn them in upon themselves. Immediately he sent them to treat massive hurts of spirit and body that festered in the world around them. . . . When he spoke of the community that would abide eternally in God's presence, it clearly would be the community of those who fed the hungry, welcomed the stranger, clothed the naked, cared for the sick, visited the prisoner.

—Stephen V. Doughty

At the same time, the open circle of the church sends its members out into the world. We engage in mission work wherever we are, in whatever we do. We exercise our gifts, not only in the company of the church, but also through the church to the world. Though we may be absent physically from our fellowship during the week, we remain spiritually connected. The life of the body constantly influences us. In countless situations, each of us enacts the mission of the church wherever we are. We bring a taste of life in the body of Christ to a world that may know only fragmentation and loneliness. We bring coherence to the chaos, generosity in place of greed to situations, compassion to the forsaken.

And the world partakes of Christ's servants as fruit that satisfies spiritual hunger. Others may be starving for the hope within us, and in their need they may gobble up our time and attention. That is what we live for. Our fruit, the life of Jesus reproduced through us, is meant to feed a hungry world. Out in daily life we give and give; we may find ourselves, as Jesus predicted, used and taken advantage of. Without God's help, we will be exhausted at the end of the week, which comes as no surprise. We need to return to the fellowship of the body to replenish our spirits through community, worship, and study. And we need to turn daily to God for renewal through prayer, meditation on scripture, and spiritual friendship.

Particular Mission

Of course, no single church, and certainly no individual, can meet all the demands of this yearning world. God has not given the whole task to any of us! Rather, different parts of the body of Christ have different functions in the universal church. Communities of Christians have different personalities and different priorities for service, just as individuals do. Some churches feel called primarily to ministries of evangelism, while others concentrate on works of concrete service. God directs some communities consistently toward global mission and others toward the local community. One church may find its identity in housing the poor while another is home to the highest art of worship in that area. Individual members naturally find themselves drawn to churches that are compatible with their gifts and sense of call.

Gustav Nelson has studied models for the church of the twenty-first century that will be both faithful to our calling and adaptable to our situation. He writes,

> The mission of the church . . . is the sum total of the life and work of each member. When a person joins a church, a congregation increases its mission; when a person leaves a church, a congregation decreases its mission. The church's mission can be defined as what church members do during the week in their life and work—in their families and in their occupations . . . [and] in their volunteer work. . . .
>
> A lean church structure sets church members free to live out their lives in the world. Active members will not spend a lot of time in the church building. They are to take up their residency in the world.[1]

The church's mission is the total of the life and work of each member. We gather together and remember who we are. We gather in worship and prayer around Jesus, our Lord and Redeemer. Then we are sent out until we meet again. And wherever we go, whatever we do, we are God's radically available people who consent to be in living reliance on Jesus Christ so that the fruit of the Spirit may be grown through us for the nurture not only of the church but also of the world. We find that the spiritual gifts we have been given for aiding this portion of the body of Christ spill over into life in the world. Though the personality and particular emphasis in every church will differ, all are called to be communities who enter the rhythm of gathering and sending, nurturing the body while always opening it to expansion. Every one of us is engaged in mission.

For example, a woman who loves dogs may discover that her passion can be a deeply meaningful ministry. She trains long hours with her faithful charges to develop dogs who can be companions for persons with AIDS, guardians of those at risk for heart attack, or visitors in nursing homes. Teachers, counselors, and lawyers enact the

Paul tells us that the gifts we operate really work because God works them (see Phil. 2:13). Because of this spiritual energy or divine grace, faithful use of our gifts is nothing short of miraculous. It goes beyond mere human abilities. The results are manifold and inestimable simply because they become the very energy of God flowing with purpose and freedom.

—Charles V. Bryant

63

compassion of Christ whenever they sit patiently and listen to the complicated, sad stories of persons whose lives have been heavy with neglect. The time they take and the care they administer are the very mission of the church.

Less directly, but not less important, all who engage their work with integrity and skill share in the work of Christ. The accountant's numbers that can be reconciled with the truth show forth the praise of God in their precision. But more, they enact the work of God who upholds the world in justice. The straight cut of wood planed in the factory echoes our Creator's delight in form and shares the church's witness that God's people trade in excellence and vigor.

In the world, we may carry groceries to the car for an older person, write letters of thanks, clean house, study botany, pray all night on our beds, drive a bus, or deliver mail. We may do all these activities as part of the mission of the body of Christ in the power of the Spirit. We may use our imaginations to consider how what we do participates in the love, goodness, beauty, and truth of God. Our attitude toward what we do can transform even drudgery into opportunity for service and praise. Everything done in the name of Jesus (even if we do not name him aloud) is part of the life of the body. But we need one another in our regular gatherings to help us remember how we are engaged in mission everywhere.

Gifts and Community

Our life together is essential for nourishing our life in Christ and enabling us to see our lives in mission. In First Peter, we read instructions for the communal life of God's people and the exercise of gifts:

> Above all, maintain constant love for one another, for love covers a multitude of sins. Be hospitable to one another without complaining. Like good stewards of the manifold grace of God, serve one another with whatever gift each of you has received. Whoever speaks must do so as one speaking the very words of God; whoever serves must do so with the strength that God supplies, so that God may be glorified in all things through Jesus Christ. To him belong the glory and the power forever and ever. Amen (4:8-11).

This brief passage highlights several concepts related to gifts:

1. As ever, love is the greater context for a consideration of gifts. Love characterizes our communion. The love of Jesus Christ for his body, the church, undergirds all that we are and do. The measure of our lives is the way we allow the love of God made known to us to flow through our lives to one another. This passage identified hospitality as a particular expression of love needed for the common life of God's people. This spiritual gift is part of Christian character. We recognize that we belong to one another and abide in one another as fellow branches in the Vine, so what we have may be freely shared.

2. As recipients of grace and gifts, we are stewards whose task is to serve one another. The Greek word *oikonomoi*, translated as "stewards," offers a rich illustration of our life together. The root of the word means "house." Stewards were servants entrusted with administering the affairs of a large household on behalf of its owner. Then as now, households required a steady inflow of goods and services to keep running. Provisions had to be secured for the members of the household, and regular maintenance and repairs made on its property. In due season, the land of the estate yielded the fruit of their labors. Good stewards managed the economy of the household with skillful efficiency so that people's needs were met and the harvest was robust.

   In Ephesians, we see this comparison between Christ's people and a household affirmed: "So then you are no longer strangers and aliens, but you are citizens with the saints and also *members of the household of God*" (Eph. 2:19, emphasis added). Being stewards of the house calls us to the realization of the grace and gifts God has given and in turn to offer them to the other members of the household. We may not minimize the resources God has given us. Through the Holy Spirit, we have access to a limitless supply of grace in Christ. Of course, we frail stewards have limits that we must respect. But

> *We will grow in grace not when we isolate ourselves from others and pay only a passing compliment to the community of Christian faith. We will grow in grace when we place ourselves regularly and faithfully in that mixed multitude of saints and sinners, of strangers and spiritual friends that we find in the average Christian congregation.*
>
> —Thomas R. Hawkins

I imagine that many of us have a far greater capacity to be conduits of grace than we have yet known. The Spirit waits for the invitation of the stewards to pour out God's love through the expression of our spiritual gifts.

As good stewards, we make an honest assessment of our resources. We acknowledge our gifts and our limits even as we rely on the boundless energy of God's love. From such a posture, we may look after the interests of the whole house, the church, and consider where and how we are called to contribute. Serving one another out of the bounty of God's love, the entire household may thrive. In this way, a needy world will receive its share of our plentiful harvest.

3. The gifts are given to each of us for the sake of one another. This is a nuance on the last point. We cannot exercise our spiritual gifts in isolation. They are not given to be hidden. Spiritual gifts are not bestowed for satellite use. The church is a communion, an organically connected body. We are not a civic organization, a political party, or a charity. We are called to be together as Christ's body on earth.

When we have discovered, by grace, our need for a constant, living reliance upon Christ Jesus the vine, our whole lives will orient around that truth. Jesus becomes the very organizing principle for all of life. He is, as the hymn says, "the heart of our own heart." Thus gathering together as the body of Christ is not optional. Worship is vital. It is the very first activity God asks of us. Praying for brothers and sisters in Christ Jesus becomes as important as taking care of our own bodies. Meeting together for study and prayer is as necessary as eating and exercising are for the body. And serving the world in the name of Christ is not optional but foundational. You and I are accountable for doing these activities.

Early in the church's life, there was only one congregation in each location, only one group of believers in a town. Today we may choose what portion of the body of Christ to join but

When we describe "Church" we like to say that it is a gift-evoking, gift-bearing community. . . . No community develops the potential of its corporate life unless the gifts of each of its members are evoked and exercised on behalf of the whole community.

—Elizabeth O'Connor

not whether we will be part of the body itself. The principle remains constant: Believers are connected organically to the body. If the church we attend is not a place where God speaks to us, if it does not provide the primary bond of fellowship in our lives, then we must overcome inertia and habit and go where we are called to be. In that portion of the body of Christ to which we are called, we may heartily, vigorously realize how necessary this community is and commit ourselves fully to its life.

We serve one another only by being connected. Of course, that happens in many places throughout the week. We exercise our gifts in the home, at work, at play, and in service. We connect with one another over the phone, around the water cooler, and on the streets. But the body must gather at least weekly in order to know its identity, to serve one another, to worship and plan and live together.

4. God calls us to exercise our gifts with a zestful, robust reliance on the Holy Spirit. The gifts are given to be used with abandon. Peter tells us that the one who speaks should do so with all urgency, passion, confidence, and joy, knowing that the words are blessed by God—not because we think we are so great, but because we trust that God will speak through us as we serve others in love through our words. If it is a word of encouragement, we may say it with confidence in God's grace. If it is a word of teaching, we may speak with the enthusiasm of trusting that God is making the divine self known. If it is a call to commitment and action, we may be bold with conviction that God has a plan for us. If it is a word of prayer, we may pray with faith that God hears and answers. If it is a tender whisper of mercy, then we say it with all the consolation of the shepherd who carries his lambs in his arms.

And Peter tells us that if our gifts are in the area of service, we should serve with all the strength God supplies. We may pick up pencils and bulletins in the sanctuary as if we

We do not have to worry about the results, since they belong to God. Our calling is to discover the spiritual ability and use it for its intended purpose. Nothing in the scheme of God's salvation is more demonstrative of obedient discipleship than our grateful reception of the gifts of the Spirit and our proper use of them.

—Charles V. Bryant

were cleaning the throne room of God. We may take a casserole to someone as if we were feeding the Lord Christ. We may make copies as if we were multiplying loaves and fish for the masses. Whether we clean a house, wash a wound, make a call, write a check, listen to a person's story, or give someone a ride to the doctor, we may do so as if Jesus himself were the recipient—because he is! And we rely on his strength to accomplish the task.

5. The ultimate purpose of the gifts is to serve one another so the church can bring the love of God to the world in such a way that glorifies God in all things through Jesus Christ. The gifts are given to be used robustly in connection to one another so that the church might be a witness to the world God loves. Spiritual gifts employed with love bring glory to God.

The point of receiving gifts is not just that we might be personally fulfilled, though we will be. It is not that our spiritual journeys will be more complete, though they will be. Discerning our call to follow Christ is not merely so we will get more out of our church experience. Gifts are given so that we might lose ourselves in service to God by serving one another and so that Jesus Christ is known and glorified throughout the world. As a by-product, all we ever yearned for will be ours. But that comes only when we lose ourselves in service to Christ.

What we are to do for God in the world and how we are to live our very lives as Christians begin and end with Jesus Christ. He calls us to himself, to a radical availability we cannot sustain on our own. But Jesus also stands in for us, giving us not only his forgiveness but also his obedience. He reproduces his life through us as we consent to his loving presence. Jesus sends the Holy Spirit to us, who comes bearing gifts for service. Employing these gifts, we grow in our oneness as Christ's body as a deeper and deeper community is created. We live, then, for "the praise of his glorious grace that he freely bestowed on us in the Beloved" (Eph. 1:6).

DAILY EXERCISES

Read the chapter for Week 5, "The Body of Christ Given for the World"; note in your journal your insights, learnings, and questions.

Listen afresh this week for the call of God to you and your church. Use this week as a time to gather up the insights, gifts, and guidance you have received from God and your small-group friends. You might want to review your notes from the previous four sessions. Articulate the call and spiritual gifts from God you celebrate for your vocation as a member of Christ's body. Remember that Christ's ministry happens in and through all that you are and do in the world, not only through organized church activities. Remember to pray for the other members of your small group as you listen together to the Lord's call to your church.

EXERCISE 1

Read 1 Corinthians 1:26-31. In light of Paul's encouragement to "consider your own call," reflect on the affirmation of gifts that you received in the last group meeting. Make a list of the gifts that the group named. Reflect on the gifts that confirm what you already knew about yourself, the gifts that surprised you, and the gifts that most challenge you. "Consider your own call" in light of these gifts.

EXERCISE 2

Read Mark 11:15-19. Meditate on this picture of Jesus in the Temple in his day. Now picture Jesus in your church today. What would Jesus see, hear, feel, affirm, and question? What would he recognize and not recognize as an expression of his life and mission? Write a dialogue with Jesus about his vision for your church and what it means to be "a house of prayer for all the nations." Listen in prayer for ways you can use your gifts to help that happen.

EXERCISE 3

Read Acts 13:1-3. The Holy Spirit who guided the church at Antioch to "set apart for me Barnabas and Saul for the work to which I have

called them" sometimes leads us to unite with others who are called to a common work. With whom (in your group or your church) are you sensing a shared mission? Toward whom is the Holy Spirit leading you for the purpose of responding to a need? Pray about your call with openness to the Holy Spirit's enabling guidance.

EXERCISE 4

Read Matthew 9:9-13. Meditate on Jesus' relationship with Matthew, the tax collector, and the way in which Matthew brought Jesus into his circle of friends. Turn your attention to your circle of friends and colleagues. How does Jesus want to participate in your relationships? In prayer, bring to mind the people you interact with daily. Sit quietly in anticipation of what Jesus might call you to do and say.

EXERCISE 5

Read Matthew 25:31-46. Meditate on the call to the church to see and respond to "the least of these" with whom Christ has united himself. What prevents you from seeing the people that Jesus names? What practices would enable you to see them? What would help you and your church to see those Jesus saw, be present to those for whom Jesus was present? Pray for eyes to see and the heart to respond.

Review your journal entries for the week in preparation for the group meeting.

Notes

Week 1   Radical Availability
1. Oswald Chambers, *My Utmost for His Highest* (London: Simpkin Marshall, 1937), 120.

Week 2   Living Reliance
1. Ray Summers, *Behold the Lamb: An Exposition on the Theological Themes in the Gospel of John* (Nashville, Tenn.: Broadman Press, 1979), 188–89.
2. Lesslie Newbigin, *The Light Has Come: An Exposition of the Fourth Gospel* (Grand Rapids, Mich.: William B. Eerdmans, 1982), 197.
3. Ibid., 198.
4. Thomas F. Torrance, *Scottish Theology* (Edinburgh: T & T Clark, 1996), 58.

Week 3   Bearing the Fruit of the Vine
1. Newbigin, *The Light Has Come*, 200.
2. Ibid.
3. Andrew Murray, *With Christ in the School of Prayer* (Old Tappan, N.J.: Fleming H. Revell, 1953), 43.
4. Ibid., 44.

Week 4   Gifts of the Spirit
1. John Calvin, *Institutes of the Christian Religion*, trans. Ford Lewis Battles, Library of Christian Classics, vol. 20 (Philadelphia: The Westminster Press, 1960), 537–41.
2. Thomas F. Torrance, *The Trinitarian Faith* (Edinburgh: T & T Clark, 1993), 228.
3. Ibid.
4. Calvin, *Institutes of the Christian Religion*, 540–41.
5. Ibid.

Week 5   The Body of Christ Given for the World
1. Gustav Nelson, "A New Model for a New Century," *Presbyterian Outlook* (30 June 1997): 7.

Sources and Authors
of Margin Quotations

Week 1   Radical Availability

Jean-Pierre de Caussade, *The Joy of Full Surrender* (Orleans, Mass.: Paraclete Press, 1986), 91.

Donald P. McNeill et al., *Compassion* (Garden City, N.Y.: Image Books, 1983), 35.

Brother Roger of Taizé, *His Love Is a Fire* (London: Geoffrey Chapman Mowbray, 1990), 58.

Week 2   Living Reliance

Howard Thurman, *Deep Is the Hunger* (Richmond, Ind.: Friends United Press, 1951), 198.

Evelyn Underhill, *The Ways of the Spirit* (New York: Crossroad, 1993), 100.

Thomas R. Hawkins, *A Life That Becomes the Gospel* (Nashville, Tenn.: Upper Room Books, 1992), 70-71.

Week 3   Bearing the Fruit of the Vine

Jacqueline McMakin with Rhoda Nary, *Doorways to Christian Growth* (Minneapolis: Winston Press, 1984), 204.

Roberta C. Bondi, *To Pray and to Love* (Minneapolis: Fortress Press, 1991), 31–32.

Andrew Murray, *With Christ in the School of Prayer* (Grand Rapids, Mich.: Zondervan, 1983), 106.

Robin Maas, *Crucified Love* (Nashville, Tenn.: Abingdon Press, 1989), 71.

Week 4   Gifts of the Spirit

Andrew Murray, *The New Life: Words of God for Young Disciples* (1998) <http://www.ccel.org/m/murray/new_life/life25.htm> (25 July 2000), chap. 22.

Ibid.

Charles V. Bryant, *Rediscovering Our Spiritual Gifts* (Nashville, Tenn.: Upper Room Books, 1991), 27.

Joan D. Chittister, *Wisdom Distilled from the Daily* (San Francisco: Harper & Row, 1990), 46.

Week 5   The Body of Christ Given for the World

Stephen V. Doughty, *Discovering Community* (Nashville, Tenn.: Upper Room Books, 1999), 110.

Bryant, *Rediscovering Our Spiritual Gifts*, 56.

Thomas R. Hawkins, *Sharing the Search* (Nashville, Tenn.: The Upper Room, 1987), 44.

Elizabeth O'Connor, *Eighth Day of Creation* (Waco, Tex.: Word Books, 1971), 8.

Bryant, *Rediscovering Our Spiritual Gifts*, 57.

Companions in Christ
Part 4 Author

 *Gerrit Scott Dawson* is the pastor of First Presbyterian Church in Baton Rouge, Louisiana, and author of three books published by The Upper Room: *Heartfelt, Writing on the Heart*, and *Called by a New Name* and has published articles in *Weavings* and *Devozine*.

Journal